Crafts From Your Favorite
Children's Stories

by KATHY ROSS

Illustrated by Elaine Garvin

The Millbrook Press   Brookfield, Connecticut

Library of Congress Cataloging-in-Publication Data
Ross, Kathy (Katharine Reynolds), 1948-
Crafts from your favorite children's stories / by Kathy Ross;
illustrated by Elaine Garvin.
p. cm.
ISBN 0-7613-1772-4 (lib. bdg.) ISBN 0-7613-1492-X (pbk.)
1. Handicraft—Juvenile literature. 2. Children's stories. [1. Handicraft.
2. Characters in literature.] I. Garvin, Elaine, ill. II. Title.
TT160 .R713 2001   745.5—dc21   00-045087

Published by The Millbrook Press, Inc.
2 Old New Milford Road
Brookfield, Connecticut 06804
www.millbrookpress.com

Contents

*For my sister "Bootsie," who can make a beautiful model
of any craft I can come up with.*
–kr

To my family, with love.
—eg

Introduction

Crafts that convert a story into a hands-on project are a wonderful way to engage young readers and listeners. They will be able to exercise their own creativity by translating characters or story concepts into tangible form.

Many of the ideas in this book can be adapted to favorite characters from several different stories. The animal-based projects, such as the Elephant Treasure Keeper or the Frog Prince Magnet, can be used with any story featuring that animal with minimal changes to the design. The basic idea behind the Henny Penny arm puppets or the poster-board figures found in the Three Bears Family craft can be adapted to many different story characters. So use this book creatively, adapting the project ideas to reflect your own favorite stories.

Kathy Ross

Johnny Gruelle wrote the first Raggedy Ann
and Andy stories in the 1920s.

Raggedy Ann Pin

Here is what you need:

scissors

1-inch (2.5-cm)
red pom-pom

ruler

white paper scrap

red and black markers

two small black beads

white glue

large-size white rickrack

small safety pin

Here is what you do:

1 Cut about one third of the fuzz
off the side of the red pom-pom.

cut

2 Cut a 1-inch (2.5-cm) circle from the white paper.

3 Use the markers to draw a smile and triangle-shaped nose on the face. Glue the two black beads on the face for eyes.

4 Glue the head to the flat cut portion on the side of the pom-pom. Glue some of the red fuzz from the pom-pom trimming on the top of the head for bangs.

5 Cut a 1-inch (2.5-cm) piece of white rickrack for a collar. Glue the top of the rickrack behind the bottom of the head.

6 Attach a safety pin to the back of the head, and Raggedy Ann is ready to wear.

You might want to make a Raggedy Andy pin, too. Just cut a circle of blue felt for a hat. Glue a strip of white ribbon around the edge for the brim. Make the head just like the one for Raggedy Ann and add the hat.

Jean De Brunhoff's wonderful stories of
Babar the elephant inspired this next project.

Elephant Treasure Keeper

Here is what you need:

newspaper to work on

blue plastic detergent
or softener bottle with
a handle

scissors

aluminum foil

masking tape

white glue

gold glitter

blue construction paper

cotton swab

two plastic wiggle eyes

small jar that will fit
inside the bottle

Here is what you do:

1 Soak the bottle in hot water to
thoroughly clean it and remove the
label. This will also soften the plastic and
make it easier to cut. Cut the bottom
part off the bottle so that the top is
left for the body of the elephant,
with the handle forming the trunk.

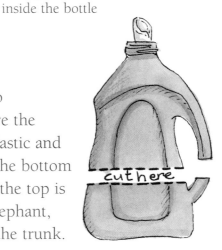

cut here

2 If you'd like a crown for your elephant, slip the inner spout out of the top of the bottle. Cover the outside of the spout with aluminum foil. Wrap the top portion of the outer rim of the crown with masking tape to create a better gluing surface. Cover the tape with glue and sprinkle it with gold glitter. Allow the glue to dry completely before slipping the spout back into the top of the bottle for a crown.

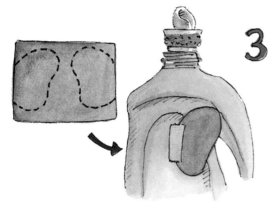

3 Cut two elephant ears from the blue paper. Use masking tape to attach one on each side of the handle that forms the trunk of the elephant.

4 Cut the cotton swab in half. Tape the two swab halves under the trunk of the elephant so that the cotton-wrapped ends stick out to form the tusks.

5 Put a small piece of masking tape on the back of each wiggle eye to create a better gluing surface. Glue the eyes to the front of the elephant above the trunk.

6 Hide the jar under the elephant.

This elephant will be happy to sit on your desk or dresser and hide secret stuff in the jar under him.

hide ➡

In Watty Piper's retelling of *The Little Engine That Could*, the positive attitude of the title character is what enables her to do what others could not.

Take the Toys up the Mountain

Here is what you need:

 newspaper to work on

large 16-inch (41-cm) square or more piece of light-colored cardboard or poster board

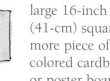 green and blue poster paint and a paintbrush

stapler

zipper long enough to reach diagonally across the cardboard

white construction paper

markers

scissors

white glue

ruler

pipe cleaner

Here is what you do:

1 Paint a slanted green hill that goes from the bottom left corner to the top right corner of the cardboard or poster board. Paint the remaining board blue for the sky.

2 Staple the ends of the zipper running up the hill, with the tab at the bottom. This will be the railroad track.

Staple

3 On the white paper use the markers to draw any scenery you would like to have around the track. Cut the drawings out and glue them on the board.

4 Use the markers to draw on the white paper a picture of the little engine pulling the cars full of toys and treats. Make the train about 5 inches (13 cm) long. Fold the paper in half and cut around the train so that you have two sides. Decorate the part that will be the other side of the train.

fold

cut line

5 String a 6-inch (15-cm) piece of pipe cleaner through the hole in the zipper tab. Wrap the ends around each other so that you have a piece about 4 inches (10 cm) long coming out from the tab.

6 Glue the two sides of the train together with the pipe cleaner in the middle so that the paper train sits on the zipper track. Starting at the bottom of the hill, you can help the little engine chug up the hill with the heavy load of toys for the children.

glue together

pipe cleaner

"I think I can, I think I can …"

Mr. Bear knew exactly what any child's mother would want for a present in Marjorie Flack's *Ask Mr. Bear*.

Bear Hug Puppet

Here is what you need:

 sturdy, 3½-inch (9-cm) paper cup

 two party blowers

masking tape

 markers

scissors

yarn in your hair color

 white glue

Here is what you do:

1 Turn the cup upside down. Poke a hole in each side of the front of the cup to insert the mouth end of the party blowers for arms. Poke a larger hole in the middle center of the back of the cup for the two ends of the blowers to come out from the cup. Use masking tape to tape the two ends of the blowers together at the back of the cup.

holes

back

2 Wrap tape around the top part of the cup above the arms to create a face area. You can leave the face the shade of the masking tape or color it in your own skin tone.

3 Use the markers to draw a face on the front of the taped area just above and between the two arms.

4 Cut bits of yarn and glue them all over the top and sides of the cup for hair.

To show what Mr. Bear suggested as a gift for mother, blow on the party blowers and watch the puppet's arms stretch out to give a big bear hug.

The griddle used to cook Paul Bunyan's breakfast was so big that the cook put the butter on his feet and skated over it to grease it.

Grease Paul Bunyan's Griddle

Here is what you need:

- 9-inch (23-cm) paper plate
- aluminum foil
- stapler
- scissors
- ruler
- hole punch
- yellow felt scrap
- paper clip
- masking tape
- white paper
- markers
- white glue
- magnet

Here is what you do:

1 Cover the top of the paper plate with the foil, folding the edges down under the paper plate. Staple the foil to the plate all the way around the edges. Trim off all the extra foil under the plate that is beyond the staples.

fold edges over plate all around

plate bottom

staples

plate top

2 Tear off a square of foil. Fold it over several times to make a 1½-inch (4-cm)-wide handle for the pan. Fold the corners of one end of the handle to round it off, then use the hole punch to punch a hole in the end of the handle. Staple the other end of the handle under the pan.

fold down corners

staples

fold in half twice   fold in thirds

3 Cut a pat of butter from the yellow felt about 1½ inches (4 cm) square.

cut line

fold

Sourdough Sam
side 1   side 2

4 Bend the inside loop of the paper clip up at a right angle to the rest of the paper clip. Cut a tiny slit to one side of the center of the felt butter pat. Slip the outer portion of the paper clip through the slit in the felt and use a tiny piece of masking tape to secure it under the felt. Leave as much of the paper clip as possible exposed for the magnet.

slit

top of butter

bottom of butter

5 Fold the white paper in half. Use the markers to draw a 1½ inch (4-cm) tall cook sideways on the paper. Cut Paul Bunyan's cook, Sourdough Sam, out on the folded paper so that you have two sides. Draw the other side of the cook on the blank side. Glue the two sides of the cook together over the paperclip sticking up through the felt square.

Put the cook and butter on the pan. Hold a magnet underneath the pan and move the magnet to move the cook around to grease the pan for Paul Bunyan's big breakfast.

In the story of *The Three Little Pigs*, the wolf keeps blowing the pigs' houses down.

Huff-and-Puff Wolf Puppet

Here is what you need:

 18 oz. (510 g) oatmeal box

 scissors

 adult brown sock

 ruler

 white glue

 large brown or black pom-pom

black marker

white construction paper scrap

 fiberfill

Here is what you do:

1 Remove the lid from the oatmeal box. Cut the bottom off the box.

2 Cut the end off the sock about 3 inches (8 cm) from the toe. Cut the 3-inch toepiece in half to make two ears for the wolf.

cut

3 Slide the cuff end of the sock over the box. Pull the end of the cuff over the open end of the box to form a mouth for the wolf. The open part of the sock should be hanging down from the other end of the box to form the neck of the wolf. This is where you will put your hand through.

4 Glue the pom-pom on the end of the box above the mouth.

5 Use the marker to draw two 1-inch (2.5-cm) eyes on the white paper. Cut the eyes out and glue them on the box above the nose.

6 Fold each ear piece in half and use glue to secure the fold. Glue the two ears on the head above the eyes.

fold

mouth

fiberfill

7 Stuff a handful of fiberfill into the box through the mouth.

To use the puppet, put your hand up through the neck to the inside of the head. Grab hold of the fiberfill. Support the head of the puppet with your other hand. As you say that the wolf "huffed" and "puffed," push the fiberfill out of the mouth slightly and then pull it back in. When he finally "blows the house down," push the fiberfill forward out of the mouth to look like a big gust of wind.

Better keep the wolf away from houses made of straw or sticks!

Because the little red hen did all the work by herself,
she also enjoyed the rewards of her work alone.

Little Red Hen Recipe Holder

Here is what you need:

white glue

red and yellow felt

corrugated box cardboard

pencil

scissors

wiggle eye

4 red feathers and 1 yellow feather

large plastic laundry soap lid

clay or Play-Doh

plastic fork

masking tape

Here is what you do:

1 Glue a piece of red felt larger than your hand to the cardboard and let it dry.

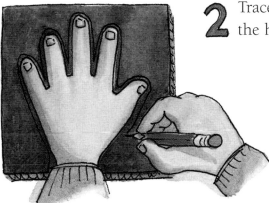

2 Trace your hand on the felt-covered cardboard. Cut the hand shape out. This will be the hen.

3 Cut a triangle beak for the hen from the yellow felt. Glue the beak on the end of the thumb. Glue on a wiggle eye above the beak.

4 Glue a red feather on each finger. Glue the yellow feather sideways across the hand for a wing.

5 Fill the inside of the plastic lid with clay or Play-Doh. Stick the handle of the fork into the center of the clay. The prongs of the fork should stick up to hold a recipe card.

masking tape

6 Put some masking tape across the side of the lid below the back side of the fork. This will create a better gluing surface for the hen. Glue the back of the hen over the tape, resting in the outer shelf portion of the lid.

The little red hen is always happy to help.

Chocolate Chip Cookies
1 bag of s...

The town mouse and the country mouse
discovered both the advantages and the disadvantages
of where each mouse lived.

Soft Sculpture Town and Country Mice

Here is what you need:

sheet of 18-inch by 12-inch (46-by 30-cm) gray construction paper

sheet of 18-inch by 12-inch (46-by 30-cm) brown construction paper

yellow, blue, pink, black, brown, and gray construction paper

stapler

scissors

white glue

ruler

two different 1-inch (2.5-cm)-wide ribbon trims

two plastic grocery bags

black yarn

black and pink 1-inch (2.5-cm) pom-poms

wheat stalk

Here is what you do:

1 The two large sheets of paper will form the heads for the two mice. Pull the sides of the sheet over each other so that the bottom of the paper comes to a point to form the nose of the mouse. Secure the paper with staples at the back where they overlap.

folds

Stuff the pocket of the folded paper with a plastic grocery bag to puff it out. Make one gray and one brown mouse head.

glue

2 Cut ears for each mouse from the matching color paper. Cut liners for the ears from the pink paper. Glue the liners on the ears, then glue the ears to the top sides of the head of each mouse.

3 Cut eyes for the mice from the black paper. Glue two eyes to the front of each mouse head.

4 Cut six 4-inch (10-cm) lengths of the black yarn. Staple the center of three strands to the back of the pointed nose of each mouse so that three strands stick out on each side for the whiskers.

5 To finish the country mouse, glue the pink pom-pom to the tip of the nose of the gray mouse head. Cut a farmer hat from the yellow paper. Glue the hat to the top of the head. Glue a strip of ribbon across the hat for a hatband. Glue a stalk of wheat sticking out of the bottom mouth area. If you don't have one, use a yellow pipe cleaner with some yarn bits glued on the end.

6 To finish the town mouse, glue the black pom-pom to the tip of the nose of the brown mouse head. Cut a hat from the blue paper. Glue the hat on the top of the head. Glue a strip of ribbon across the hat for a hatband.

Which mouse would you like to be ... the town mouse or the country mouse?

In *The Tale of Peter Rabbit* by Beatrix Potter, little Peter gets into lots of trouble when he disobeys his mom!

Hide Peter in the Watering Can Puppet

Here is what you need:

golf tee

paper cup about 3½ inches (9 cm) tall

masking tape

aluminum foil

12-inch (30-cm) black pipe cleaner

two flexible straws

white glue

two large cotton balls

scissors

black and brown markers

hole punch

pink and white paper scraps

ruler

black yarn

blue felt scrap

gold sequin

Here is what you do:

1 To make the watering can, poke the golf tee into the side of the paper cup at an angle to look like a spout. Use masking tape to secure it on the inside of the cup. Cover the cup and golf tee with aluminum foil.

2 Fold the black pipe cleaner in half and twist the two halves together to make a handle for the watering can. Poke the two ends of the handle into the opposite side of the cup from the spout. Secure the ends inside the cup with masking tape.

3 To make Peter Rabbit, use masking tape to tape the two flexible straws together just below the bends.

4 Rub glue over the taped area. Slide the two cotton balls over the taped area by pushing the ends of the straws through the center of each cotton ball. The bottom cotton ball will form the body of the rabbit and the top one the head, with the two straws sticking out at the top for ears. Spread the two ears apart slightly.

5 Cover the front and back of each ear with a flat piece of masking tape. Do not wrap the tape around the ear, but rather allow the front and back tape to stick to each other on each side of the straw. Trim the tape so that it is pointed at the top like a rabbit's ear.

6 Use the brown marker to color the ears and the cotton ball head brown.

7 Punch eyes from the white paper. Use the black marker to give each eye a pupil. Glue the eyes to the head of the rabbit.

8 Cut a 2-inch (5-cm) length of black yarn. Knot the yarn in the center, then trim the ends to make whiskers about as wide as the rabbit's face. Unravel each strand of yarn. Punch a nose from the pink paper. Glue the whiskers to the face, then glue the pink nose over the center of the whiskers.

9 Cut a rectangle of blue felt wide enough to cover the rabbit's body and long enough to wrap around it for a little jacket. Glue the jacket wrapped around the body of the rabbit. Glue the gold sequin to the front of the jacket for a button.

10 Poke a hole in the bottom center of the watering can. Slide the end of the two straws through the hole from the inside of the cup, so that you can pop Peter Rabbit in and out of the watering can.

Quick! Help Peter hide! Here comes Mr. McGregor.

In *The Wizard of Oz*, Dorothy and Toto went to Oz in a spinning house.

Spinning House

Here is what you need:

scissors

½-gallon (2-liter) milk carton

ruler

string

large spool

white, blue, and red construction paper

white glue

markers

Here is what you do:

1 Cut the top off the milk carton about 3 inches (8 cm) down from the end of the spout. This will be the house.

2 Cut a 5-foot (1.5-meter) length of string. Poke a small hole in two opposite corners of the house, just below the end of the folded-in spout. Thread one end of the string through the hole on one side, into the house, and out the other hole. Thread the end of the string through the spool, then tie the two ends together.

3 Cut a strip of white paper to wrap around the outside of the house to cover it and overlap at each end. Glue the strip in place over the sides of the house. Cut a triangle of white paper to fit under each side of the roof to cover any print on the milk carton. Cut a piece of blue paper to fold over the top of the spout to cover it and hang out over each side to form a roof. Cut a chimney for the house from the red paper. Glue the chimney to the top of the roof.

4 Use markers and cut paper to add doors, windows, and any other detail you might want on the house.

To make your house spin off to Oz, hold the spool with one hand and twist the house around several times on the end of the string with your other hand. When you let the house go, it will spin on the end of the string.

Which of the three bears would you like to be?

Three Bears Family

Here is what you need:

scissors

markers

three large sheets of
white poster board

Here is what you do:

1 Cut a hole slightly larger than
your head in the top center of the
poster board. You might want to use a
plate as a pattern and trace around it.

2 Cut a smaller hole on each side of
the poster board just below the
center for your hands. You might want
to use a large cup to trace around for a
pattern. If the holes are not quite big
enough for your hands, just trim a bit
more off the edges until they feel right.

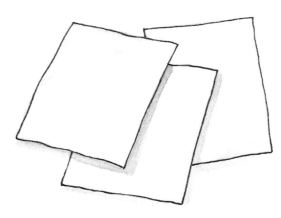

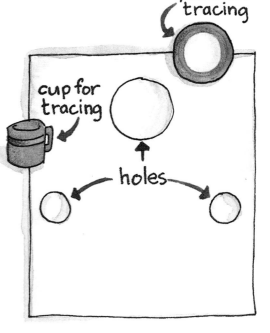

plate for
tracing

cup for
tracing

holes

3 Choose which bear you are making and use the markers to draw the bear on the poster board. The hole for your head should just be outlined and given bear ears. Add clothes below, with the arms ending in the two holes where your hands come through. Just draw the start of the legs where your own legs will come down to provide the legs for the character.

To use the bear costume, just put your hands through the back of the holes and peek through the head hole.

All you need is someone to be Goldilocks, and you can put on a play.

Peter Pan was a young boy who could fly!

Flying Peter Pan

Here is what you need:

newspaper to work on

masking tape

paper toy airplane

green poster paint and a paintbrush

ruler

scissors

white and green construction paper

white glue

red feather

markers

Here is what you do:

1 If the body of the airplane is Styrofoam rather then cardboard you will need to cover it with one thin layer of masking tape in order to paint it. Do not overlap the tape as this will add extra weight to the airplane and it will not fly.

2 Paint the airplane green. This will be the body of the flying Peter Pan.

3 Cut two identical 1½-inch (4-cm) circles from the white paper. Glue them together over the front tip of the airplane for the head. Cut two green triangles for the hat. Glue them together over the top of the head. Glue the red feather to one side of the hat.

fold paper in half to cut two of each

4 Draw a face on each side of the head with the markers.

5 Cut two hands from the white paper. Glue the end of a hand under the tip of each wing of the plane to make them look like outstretched arms.

fold

Fly Peter Pan just as you would a toy airplane. Don't throw him too hard or he may end up in Never Never Land.

When Pinocchio told a lie his nose would grow longer.

Growing Nose Pinocchio Puppet

Here is what you need:

newspaper to work on

2-inch (5-cm) Styrofoam ball

light brown poster paint and a paintbrush

ballpoint pen

scissors

green, white, black, and red construction paper

ruler

white glue

stapler

red feather

unsharpened pencil

Here is what you do:

1 Paint the Styrofoam ball brown and let it dry.

2 Use the pen to poke a hole straight through the center of the Styrofoam ball. This will be where the unsharpened pencil will go through to form the growing nose.

3 Cut two circles for eyes from the white paper. Cut two smaller circles from the black paper for pupils and glue one in the center of each eye. Glue the eyes on the Styrofoam ball head just above the nose hole.

4 Cut a smile from the red paper. Glue the smile on the head under the nose hole.

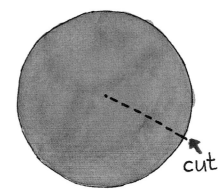

cut   staple

5 Cut a 4-inch (10-cm) circle from the green paper. Cut a slit from the edge to the center of the circle. Wrap one side of the cut circle over the other, overlapping by about 3 inches (8 cm), and staple the sides together to form a cone-shaped hat. Glue the red feather on one side of the hat.

To make Pinocchio's nose grow when he tells a lie, just push the pencil forward through the nose hole. Don't forget to always tell the truth!

Henny Penny was a little hen that
mistakenly thought the sky was falling.

Hand Wings Henny Penny

Here is what you need:

 newspaper to
work on

scissors

ruler

 corrugated
cardboard

 red poster paint
and a paintbrush

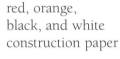 red, orange,
black, and white
construction paper

 white glue

 red feathers

Here is what you do:

1 Cut a 15-inch (38-cm) circle from the
cardboard. Cut a 3-inch (8-cm) circle
out of the middle of the circle on each side
so that your hands can slip through the
holes to become the wings for Henny Penny.

2 Paint the front of the cardboard
circle red.

3 Cut a 10-inch (25-cm)-tall head for the hen from the red construction paper. Cut eyes from the white paper and pupils for the eyes from the black paper. Glue a pupil in the center of each eye and glue the eyes on the head of the hen. Fold a piece of the orange paper in half and cut a triangle beak on the fold. Glue the back triangle only of the folded beak to the head of the hen so that the beak looks open.

fold

glue bottom only

4 Glue red feathers along the neck of the hen. Glue one red feather at the top of the head.

5 Glue the head to the top section of the cardboard.

fold

6 Cut two legs from orange construction paper. Glue them to the bottom of the cardboard.

Put your hands through the holes and flap them like wings as you tell all your friends that "the sky is falling."

You can use this same idea to make all the characters in the story of Henny Penny. If you make Foxy Loxy, just put socks over your hands to make them look like paws.

Cocky Locky   Ducky Lucky   Goosey Loosey   Turkey Lurkey   Foxy Loxy

The spoiled princess in the story *The Frog Prince* did not
want to keep her promise to the frog.

Frog Prince Magnet

Here is what you need:

newspaper to
work on

green poster paint
and a paintbrush

masking tape

two wooden
ice-cream spoons

scissors

two wiggle eyes

three green twist ties

green and yellow
felt scraps

thin red ribbon

gold jingle bell

white glue

sequins

piece of pipe cleaner

piece of sticky-back
magnet

Here is what you do:

1 With the bowl of one spoon as the bottom
portion of the frog, glue one twist tie
across the center to form the arms. Glue two
more twist ties hanging down from the bottom to form the legs. Glue the second spoon over the first, with the
bowl of the second spoon at the top
of the frog for the head.

Glue
top
spoon
to
bottom
spoon

Bottom
Spoon

2 Paint the frog green.

3 Cut flipper hands and feet for the frog from the green felt. Glue a flipper to the end of each arm and leg.

4 Cut a crown for the frog from the yellow felt. Glue the crown to the top of the head of the frog. Decorate the crown with sequins for jewels.

5 Put a square of masking tape on the back of each wiggle eye to create a better gluing surface. Glue the two wiggle eyes to the head of the frog just below the crown. Cut a snip of the red ribbon to glue on for the mouth.

6 The jingle bell will be the gold ball the frog retrieved for the princess. Thread the piece of pipe cleaner through the hanger at the top of the jingle bell. Wrap the two ends of the pipe cleaner around the wrist of the frog so that it looks like the frog is holding the gold ball. Trim off any extra pipe cleaner.

7 Put a piece of sticky-back magnet on the back of the frog.

Stick the frog on your refrigerator and remember that it is important for you to keep your promises.

I'll keep my promises ☺

The gingerbread boy hopped right out
of the oven and ran away.

Running Gingerbread Boy

Here is what you need:

brown and green
construction paper

pencil

thin craft ribbon
spool

scissors

white glue

markers

rickrack trim

12-inch (30-cm)
pipe cleaner

cellophane tape

stapler

Here is what you do:

1 Fold the green paper in half. Trace around the ribbon spool on the paper. Cut out the traced circle on the folded paper so that you get two circles. Glue a circle over each side of the ribbon spool to cover it. Use the pencil to poke a hole through the paper on each side to reopen the hole in the center of the spool.

trace around

fold

glue

2 On the brown paper draw one leg for the gingerbread boy as tall as the distance from the center of the spool to the outside edge. Cut the leg out and use it as a pattern to make a total of eight identical legs. Glue four legs on each side of the spool, evenly spaced, with the tops meeting at the outside edge of the hole at the center of the spool.

pattern

side 1
side 2

3 Fold the brown paper in half. Draw the head and body of the gingerbread boy sideways, making him about 4 inches (10 cm) tall. Do not draw arms or legs. Make the body as wide as the ribbon spool. Cut the body out with the paper folded so that you get two sides of the gingerbread boy. Cut an arm for each side and glue them in place.

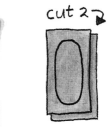

4 Use the markers to give each side of the ginger-bread boy a face. Decorate each side with rickrack to look like frosting.

5 Poke the pipe cleaner through the hole at the center of the spool. Fold each end of the pipe cleaner up, making sure the bend keeps the sides of the pipe cleaner from rubbing on the sides of the spool. Tape one side of the gingerbread boy to the pipe cleaner on each side of the spool so that the bottom of the body is just covering the hole in the center of the spool. Make sure the feet and the body are all facing in the same direction. Twist together the ends of the pipe cleaner above the head to make a handle. Staple the two sides of the head on both sides of the pipe cleaner.

To make the gingerbread boy run, hold onto the handle at the top and roll the spool across a table. You may need to adjust the pipe cleaner now and then to keep it from rubbing on the sides of the spool and slowing the gingerbread boy down.

"Run, run, run, as fast as you can ..."

The tortoise showed the hare that slow
and sure can win the race.

Racing Tortoise and Hare

Here is what you need:

 2 small toy cars

 white glue

 scissors

masking tape

 green, brown, black, and white construction paper

 black and pink markers

hole punch

fiberfill

tiny pink pom-pom

larger white pom-pom

Here is what you do:

1 Cover the top of each of the cars with a strip of masking tape to create a better gluing surface.

2 To make the hare, glue fiberfill to the top of one car. Pull some fiberfill down over each side of the car, but do not obstruct the wheels. This will be the body of the hare. Cut two rabbit ears from the white paper. Color the centers of each ear with the pink marker. Glue the ears to the top front of the car. Punch eyes from the black paper and glue them on the front of the car. Glue the pink pom-pom below the eyes for a nose. Glue the white pom-pom on the back of the car for the tail.

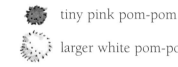

3 To make the tortoise, cut a 2½-inch (6-cm) circle from the green paper. Cut four evenly spaced ½-inch (1-cm) slits around the outside of the circle. Create a shell for the tortoise by folding each slit over itself and securing it from behind with masking tape. Put fiberfill inside the shell and secure it with strips of masking tape across the opening.

outside ↘

overlap

inside ↘

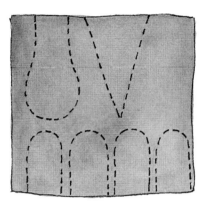

Cut a head, four legs, and a tail from the brown paper.

Glue the head sticking out from the front of the car, the tail from the back, and two legs sticking out from each side. Glue the shell over the top of the car. Give the tortoise a face and details on the shell using the black marker.

This tortoise and hare will race best on a bare floor.

On your mark, get set ... GO!

Bambi, by Felix Salten, tells the story of a little fawn and his forest friends.

Bambi Puppet

Here is what you need:

lunch bag

scissors

1-inch (2.5-cm) black pom-pom

fiberfill

white glue

black and brown construction paper

white poster paint

Here is what you do:

1 Turn the bag so that the bottom flap is at the top. Fold the two corners of the flap in and secure them with glue to form the face of the puppet.

fold corners under

2 Cut two ears from the brown paper. Glue an ear on each side of the head. Cut two eyes from the black paper and glue them in place below the ears. Glue the black pom-pom on the bottom edge of the flap, between the two folded edges, for the nose.

3 Glue a thin layer of fiberfill on the front of the bag for the front of the fawn.

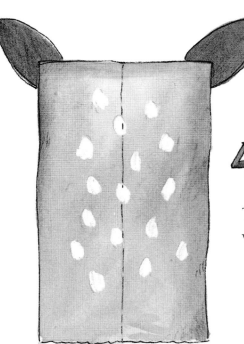

4 Turn the bag over. Dip your finger in the white paint and give the fawn fingerprint spots on the back.

To use the puppet, just slip your hand inside the bag and work the flap head up and down.

The white spots help a fawn hide from danger in the woods. Better give him lots of them!

In the Ukranian folktale, *The Mitten*, so many animals crawled into the mitten that it finally burst.

Bursting Mitten

Here is what you need:

 scissors

two identical 16-oz. (454-g) sturdy plastic cups

wooden tongue depressor stick

 masking tape

 large knit mitten

 seven or more pom-poms of various sizes and colors

hole punch

 yarn pieces

paper scraps

 white glue

Here is what you do:

1 Cut a hole in the bottom of one cup to slide the stick through. Cut an identical hole in the second cup. Cut the top off the second cup so that it is about 2 inches (5 cm) tall.

2 Put the stick through the bottom of the short cup so that about 1 inch (2.5 cm) sticks up inside the cup. Secure the stick with masking tape. Slide the other end of the stick down into the large cup and all the way out so that the small cup is at the bottom of the large cup. Put the cups inside the upper part of the mitten with the stick down in the mitten.

3 Use the various pom-poms to make the faces of animals to go in the mitten. Different tellers of the story use different animals, so make whatever you want. Add facial details with cut and punched paper and yarn bits. Make at least seven. You can make more if you have room in the cup.

mouse   frog   rabbit   fox   wolf   wild boar   bear

To use the bursting mitten, keep adding pom-pom animals as the story is told. When the last animal crawls in and bursts the mitten, hold the mitten firmly with both hands and hit the stick straight down on the floor. The inner cup will push up and throw all the animals out of the mitten, just like in the story.

In the Aesop's fable *The Crow and the Pitcher*, a smart crow solves the problem of how to get a drink.

Smart Crow Puppet

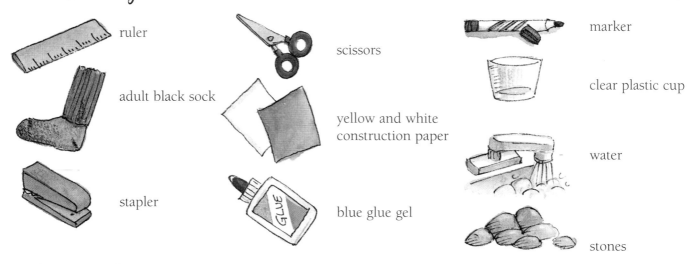

Here is what you need:

ruler

adult black sock

stapler

scissors

yellow and white construction paper

blue glue gel

marker

clear plastic cup

water

stones

Here is what you do:

1 The black sock will be the body of the crow. Turn about 3 inches (8 cm) of the sock toe in on itself to form a mouth. Separately staple the fold on the heel side and top side of the sock.

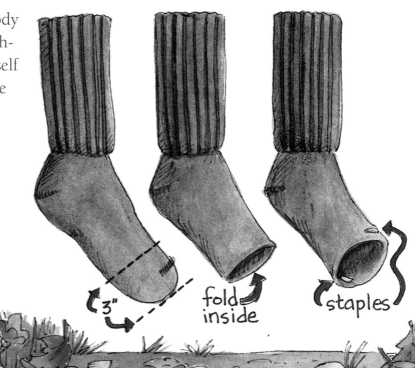

3"

fold inside

staples

2 Cut two identical 3-inch (8-cm) triangles for the top and bottom beak of the crow from the yellow paper. Glue a triangle beak over each staple on the top and bottom of the mouth.

3 Cut two eyes from the white paper. Use the marker to draw a pupil in the center of each eye. Glue the eyes on the heel side of the sock, just above the beak.

Fill the cup half full of water for the pitcher. Put your hand inside the crow puppet with your fingers on each side of the folded-in mouth. Have the crow keep picking up stones and dropping them in the water until the level rises enough to get a drink.

What a smart bird!

About the Author and Artist

Twenty-five years as a teacher and director of nursery school programs have given Kathy Ross extensive experience in guiding young children through craft projects. Among the more than thirty-five craft books she has written are CRAFTS FOR ALL SEASONS, MAKE YOURSELF A MONSTER, THE BEST BIRTHDAY PARTIES EVER, CRAFTS FROM YOUR FAVORITE FAIRY TALES, and CRAFTS FROM YOUR FAVORITE CHILDREN'S SONGS.

Elaine Garvin designs and illustrates greeting cards and she has illustrated more than twenty children's books over the past ten years. A member of the Society of Children's Book Writers and Illustrators and the Graphic Artists Guild, she lives and works in the Phoenix, Arizona, area.

If you would like to know more about the author or the artist of this book, visit them at their Web sites.

www.kathyross.com
www.elainegarvin.com